My sunglasses and me

(A fun way to understand how and why this Autistic child used sunglasses)

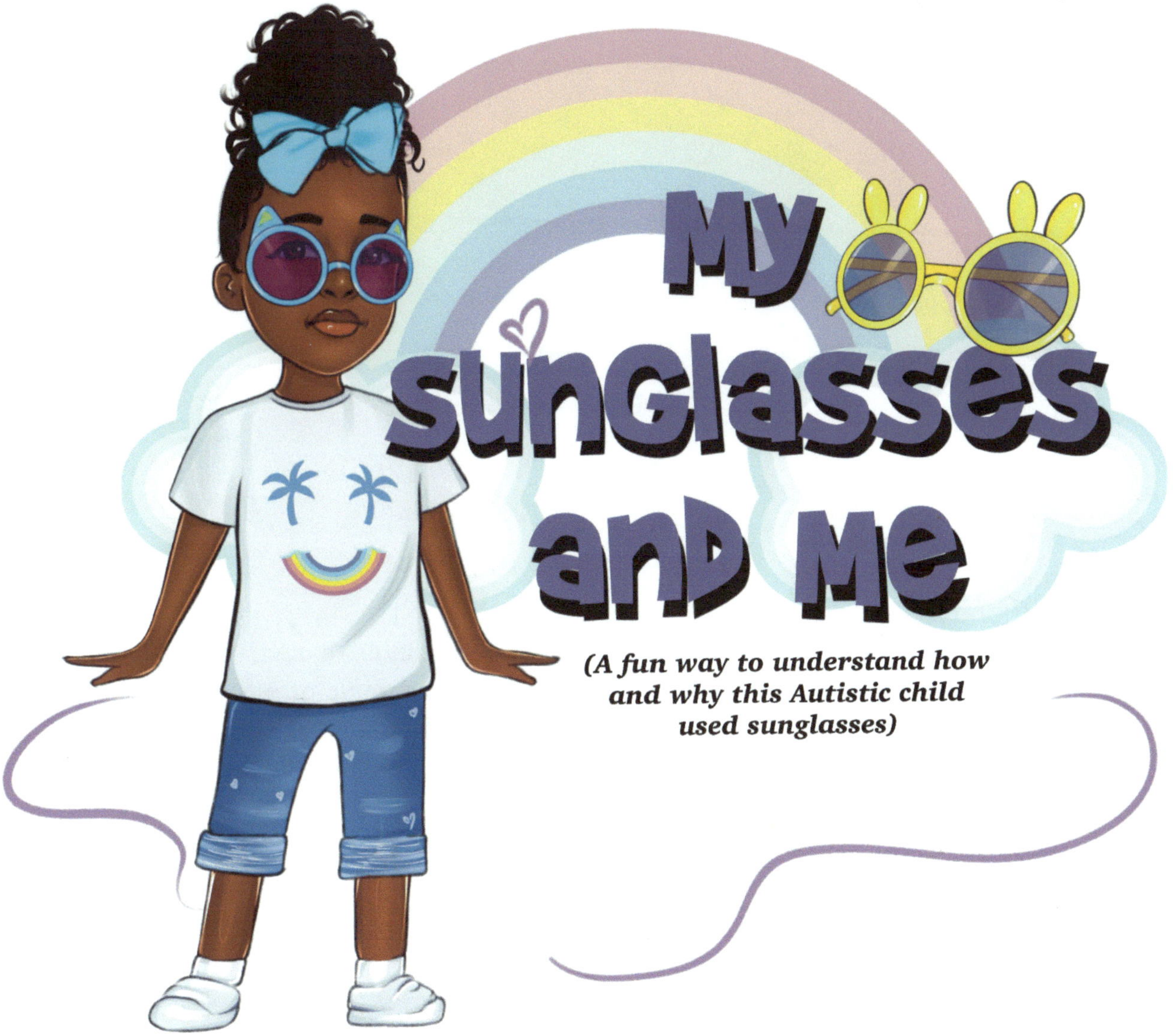

By: Tabitha Ackers

Illustrated by: Nmugha Chimezie (carniels_art)

Illustrated by Nmugha Chimezie (carniels_art)

Hardcover: ISBN: 978-1-960853-44-8

Paperback: ISBN: 978-1-960853-55-4

eBook: 978-1-960853-45-5

Liberation's Publishing - Columbus, MS

Harper
kallie's
Club

I have Autism and my sunglasses
are helpful every day.
I wear my sunglasses, so I will
not appear mean or rude.
When people talk with me, I do
not feel so good when looking
them in the eyes.

I also hear better when I do not look them in their eyes. It allows me to focus more effectively when talking with others.

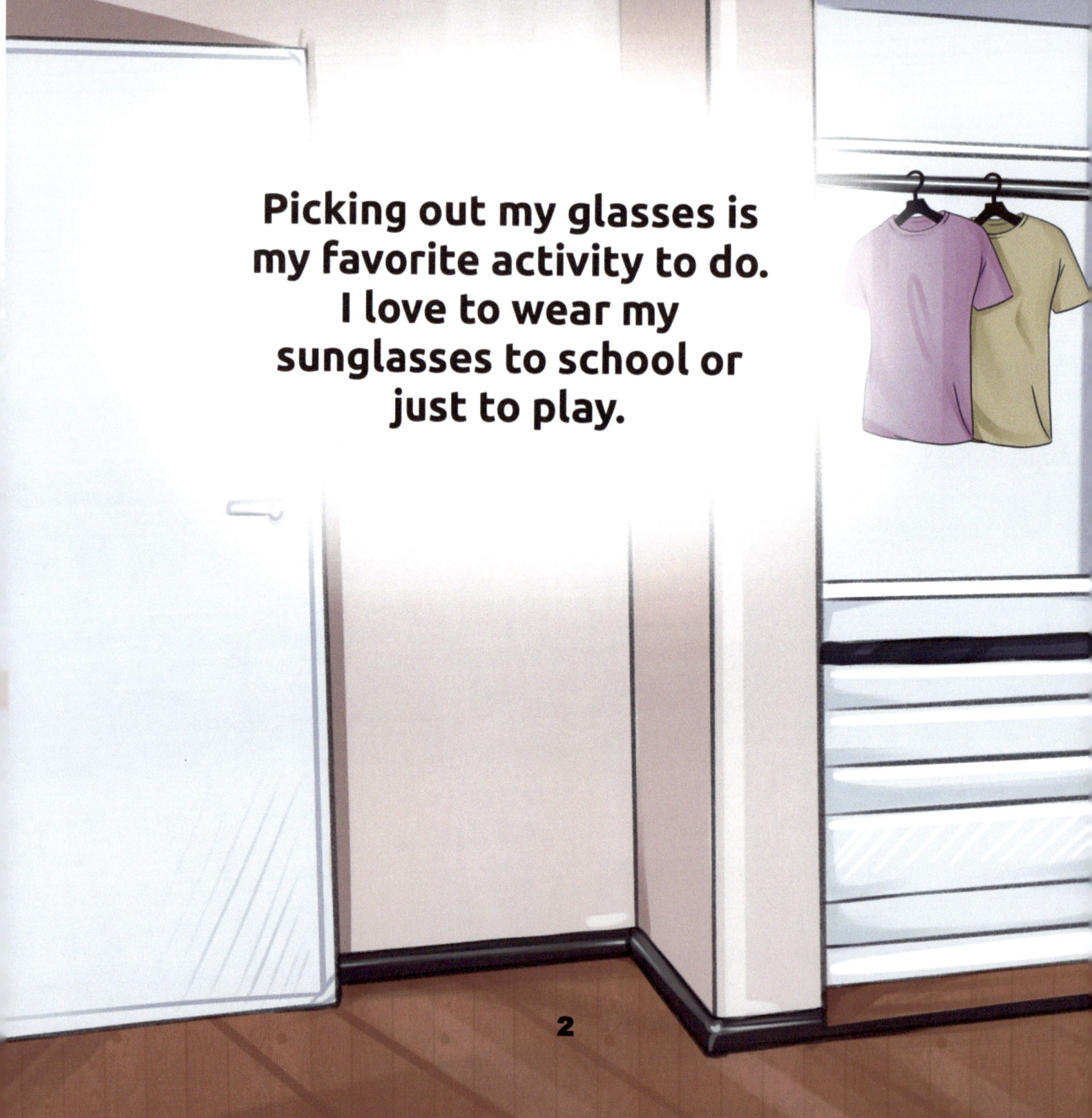

Picking out my glasses is my favorite activity to do. I love to wear my sunglasses to school or just to play.

2

3

I can mix them or match them to my
outfits for the day.
With my hair bows, shirt, and shoes.
It is my desire to express my
feelings for the day.

I have orange, red,
yellow, purple, and blue.
I may have to choose
two.

5

The sun is shining
bright today.
I am ready to go play
and start my day.

7

Hey everyone!

My sunglasses are one of the best parts of my day. I talk, jump, sing, and play. I feel comfortable in my own way.

My sunglasses make me feel so cool even on a sunny day!